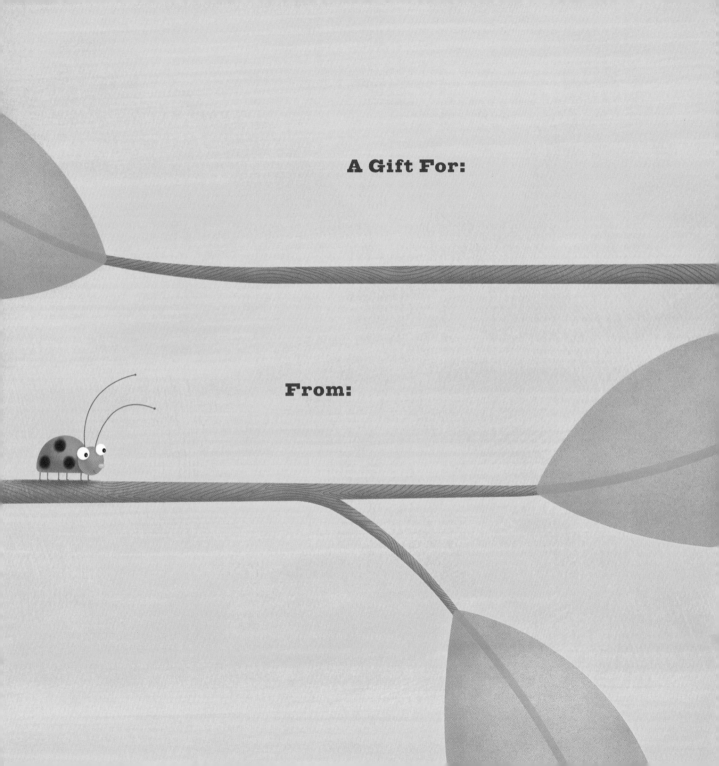

A Gift For:

From:

How to Use Your Interactive Storybook & Story Buddy:

1. Press your Story Buddy's ear to start.
2. Read the story aloud in a quiet place. Speak in a clear voice when you see the highlighted phrases.
3. Listen to your buddy respond with several different phrases throughout the book.

Clarity and speed of reading affect Watson's response. He may not always respond to young children.

Watch for even more Interactive Storybooks and Story Buddies. Available only at Hallmark. For more information, visit us on the Web at www.Hallmark.com/StoryBuddy.

Copyright © 2011 Hallmark Licensing, Inc.

Published by Hallmark Books,
a division of Hallmark Cards, Inc.,
Kansas City, MO 64141
Visit us on the Web at www.Hallmark.com.

Editors: Emily Osborn and Megan Langford
Art Director: Kevin Swanson
Designer: Mary Eakin
Production Artist: Dan Horton

ISBN: 978-1-59530-357-8
KOB8004
Printed and bound in China
OCT10

BOOK 3

Watson and the Case of The Little Lost Caterpillar

By **Keely Chace** | Illustrated by **Karla Taylor**

Hallmark
GIFT BOOKS

One sunny day, a clever raccoon was sniffing around in a wild lilac bush. Even though the flowery smell made him sneeze, Watson needed to keep his sniffer in tip-top shape so he could track down clues. You see, Watson loved solving mysteries.

When a baby deer's spots went missing or a smelly smell needed investigating, the other animals knew exactly who to call. And before they could say "April showers," Watson would be on the case.

Watson had just finished sniffing practice when
he heard a big, noisy ruckus. "What's that?" he
thought. "Could it be a mys—?"

Before he even finished his thought, a nearby
squirrel cried out, "Watson! Somebody call Watson!"

Watson followed the voices of many forest animals
until he found himself face-to-face with a very sad-looking
Lola Ladybug.

Lola blew her nose into her tiny hanky and cried,
"Watson, I could really use your help!"

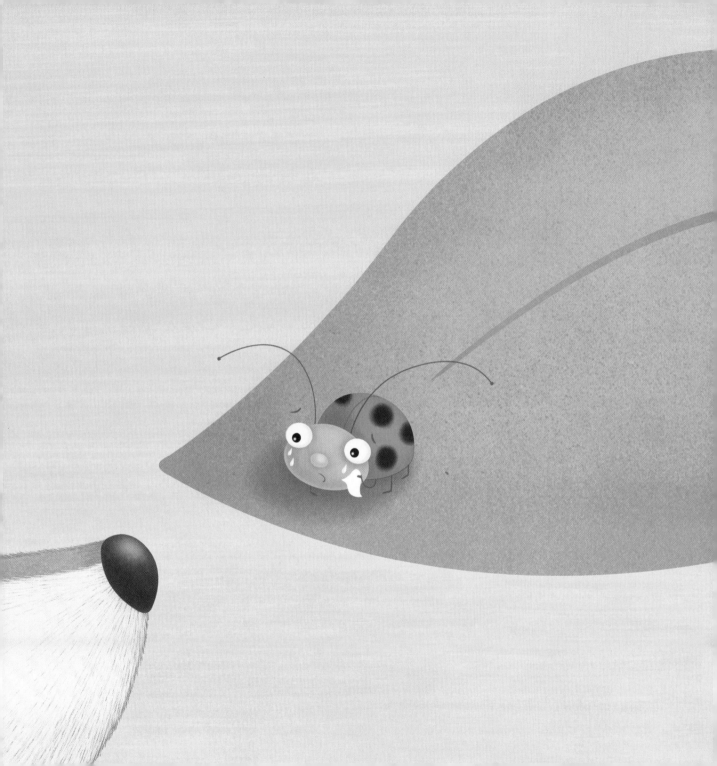

"It's awful," sniffled Lola. "I can't find my best
friend, Kip Caterpillar."

"There, there," said Watson. "Tell me everything."

"Well," said Lola, "he's long and stripy, and he said
he'd have a big surprise next time I saw him, but that
was days ago! Oh, Watson, can you help me find Kip?"

Watson thought about his first clue. Lola
had said Kip was long and stripy . . .

Long and stripy? Hey! Watson had just
seen something long and stripy. Where was it?
He looked left and right. Nothing. He looked
straight ahead. Nothing. Then Watson looked
behind himself, and that's when he spied it!
It was . . .

. . . his tail.

Watson saw it wasn't a caterpillar.

Watson thought about his next clue. Kip said he would have a big surprise for Lola. Where would a caterpillar get a surprise?

Just then, Watson spotted Holly Hummingbird over in a clump of wildflowers. Aha! Kip must have gone to pick some for Lola. And caterpillars were slow—it might have taken him days! So Watson wandered over to the flowers, where he found not one, not two, but **THREE** caterpillars. This mystery would be solved in no time!

But when Watson showed the caterpillars to Lola, she just sniffled and shook her head. None of them were Kip, and one of them . . .

Well, now Watson saw it wasn't a caterpillar.

It was just Waldo Worm, covered in streaky, stripy dirt. Whoopsie! Watson needed a new clue.

Just then, Waldo spoke up. "I saw Kip Caterpillar a few days ago," he said. "He was headed for a big, big tree."

A clue! Watson knew he'd picked up Waldo for a reason.

"Oh, please!" said Lola. "Watson, can you help me find Kip?"

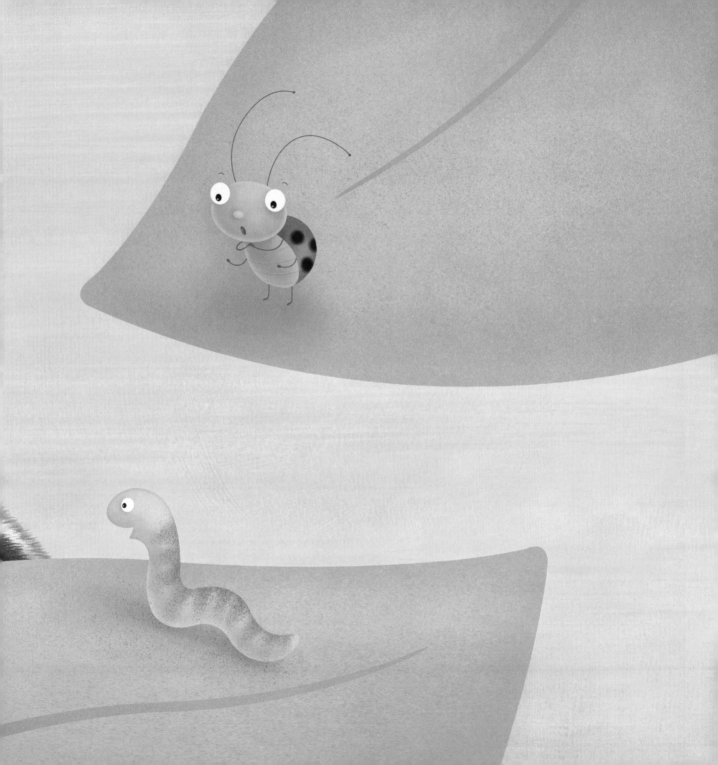

Determined to find Kip, Watson and Lola followed Waldo to the biggest tree in the forest. Watson gave the tree a long sniff, just like he'd practiced. It smelled big, all right—but he couldn't decide if it smelled like caterpillar.

"Are you here, Kip?" called Watson.

"Who?" said someone up in the branches.

It was Harriet Hawk. Watson asked her if she'd
seen a caterpillar, but Harriet giggled and said there
was no way a little caterpillar could be in such a big,
big tree.

Harriet had a point. Watson was just turning to
go sniff someplace smaller for his next clue when he
spied the strangest leaf. Instead of flat, it was fat.
Also, it was moving! What kind of leaf moved?

Then suddenly, it happened! Something popped out
of the funny fat leaf! Watson saw it wasn't a caterpillar.

It was a butterfly! It crawled out onto the
branch and flapped its pretty wings a few times.
Then it looked down and called, "Lola, hi! It's me,
Kip! I told you I'd have a big surprise next time I
saw you!" He fluttered down and gave Lola a big hug.

Lola was surprised—and very happy to have
her friend back. "Watson, you did it!" she said.
"You found Kip! Oh, Watson, thank you!"

But no thanks were needed. After all,
Watson loved solving mysteries.

Did you have fun solving
this mystery with Watson?
Tell us about it!

Please send your comments to:
Hallmark Book Feedback
P.O. Box 419034
Mail Drop 215
Kansas City, MO 64141

Or e-mail us at:
booknotes@hallmark.com